Would We
Still Be

New Issues Poetry & Prose

Editor	Nancy Eimers
Contributing Editor	Bill Olsen
Managing Editor	Kimberly Kolbe
Assistant Editors	Sara Lupita Olivares & Alyssa Jewell

New Issues Poetry & Prose
The College of Arts and Sciences
Western Michigan University
Kalamazoo, MI 49008

First Edition, 2021.

ISBN-13   978-1-936970-70-4 (paperbound)

Library of Congress Cataloging-in-Publication Data:
Knippen, James Henry
Would We Will Still Be/James Henry Knippen
Library of Congress Control Number: 2020940736

Art Director	Nick Kuder
Designer	Nicole Wieferich
Production Manager	Paul Sizer
	The Design Center, Frostic School of Art
	College of Fine Arts
	Western Michigan University
Printing:	Books International

Would We
Still Be

James Henry Knippen

New Issues Press

WESTERN MICHIGAN UNIVERSITY

—for Elizabeth

—for my family

Table of Contents

Acknowledgments

Thank you to the editors of the following journals in which these poems, sometimes in earlier versions, first appeared:

1110: "Pillow Talk"
1913 A Journal of Forms: "Ghosts Love Windows"
32 Poems: "Moon"
Boston Review: "Poem" (p. 13)
burntdistrict: "Dinner Table Conversations" sects. 2 and 3
Cimarron Review: "Porch," "The Moon"
The Cincinnati Review: "The Body before the Judgment"
Colorado Review: "When," "Dinner Table Conversations" sect. 4
Crazyhorse: "Tercets for Fear," "Butterfly"
Denver Quarterly: "Couplets for Hopelessness," "Thistle"
DIAGRAM: "Sonnet"
Gulf Coast: "Beggars," "Lilies"
Hayden's Ferry Review: "Voices"
Interrupture: "Dinner Table Conversations" sects. 5 and 6, "Hallway"
Kenyon Review Online: "Poem" (p. 7) and "Portents"
The Missouri Review Online: "Oaks"
Smartish Pace: "Answers"
Softblow: "The Cat," "Window"
Third Coast: "The Sound of Injured Rabbits"
West Branch: "Garden on the Windowsill"
West Branch Wired: "Rhymes for the Cat's Ashes"

"A Wren" appears at the 92nd Street Y Unterberg Poetry Center's website: www.92y.org/poetry.

For your mentorship, friendship, inspired thinking, and profound commitment to the poems themselves, thank you Kathleen Peirce.

For shaping and caring for my poetry in so many ways, thank you Trey Moody, Roger Jones, Cyrus Cassells, and Ben Doller. For your continued support of my writing, and for your generosity and hospitality when I first decided to pursue poetry, thank you Cole Swensen.

Much gratitude to Traci Brimhall for selecting this manuscript, and to Nancy Eimers, Kim Kolbe, and the editorial and design team at New Issues Poetry & Prose.

For opening my eyes to forum analysis, which led to early and continued successes in publishing, thank you Deb Balzhiser.

For your insight, encouragement, and support along the way, thank you John, Luisa, Sara, Lev, Will, Mary, Colin, and the Texas State University creative writing program. Thanks also to Suzanne Richardson, Daniel Shank Cruz, and G.C. Waldrep.

I am grateful to the 92nd Street Y Unterberg Poetry Center and especially to Ricardo Alberto Maldonado, Sophie Herron, and Timothy Donnelly.

For championing my life in poems early on, thank you Christine Bryant, Tyehimba Jess, and Christine Bodine.

Thanks to Claire Wahmanholm for asking for the moon.

For cultivating a beautiful community built around poetry and for including me in it, thank you Jasmine V. Bailey, George David Clark, Eduardo C. Corral, Brandon Courtney, Shira Dentz, Benjamin Garcia, and Octavio Quintanilla.

I am indebted to my family. Thank you for your unending support and for fostering from the very beginning an environment in which my imagination would flourish.

Finally, thank you, Elizabeth, for loving me, for being the best reader of my work, and for always challenging me to be a better poet.

Poem

Like a yellow light means drive faster.
Like the metal stem of an umbrella
makes one feel larger in a lightning storm.
Like night makes passages vaster.
Like death makes words mean more.

Like rain fills footprints a fox left in silt.
Like one's lips become lampreys
smuggling purple blood in death's wake.
Like love is the word most likely to wilt.
Like the heart is dragged like a lake.

Like a good river hugs its cities to sleep.
Like the nearest star to the darkness
of shark eyes kisses the lilies alive.
Like a slaughterhouse worships its guise of trees.
Like a ghost bites the end of a line.

Like a hawk forsakes a starling's feathers.
Like a closet trapped inside a ghost
opens and shuts like an aortic valve.
Like a song despises the cage it weathers.
Like a fractured bone forgives itself.

Like a good moon carves its oceans askew.
Like the human eyes sculpted into a whale
sink back to a deeper, older dark.
Like hope dismantles the gatehouse in you.
Like the dead drag the moats of the heart.

Moon

Wet moon on bluestem, if sound
is enough. If sound is enough,

trillium tryst. Mouth full of
dark roses, if image is enough. If

image is enough, weeping gladiolus.
Frangipani at dusk, if fragrance

is enough. If flavor is enough,
moonseed paralysis. Gold shadow

of monkshood, if faith is enough.
If touch equals faith, moons do

not exist. Rose shadows wither
when the hedge is on fire. If love

is enough, chrysanthemum kiss.
Blue light licks the lakeshore

if the moon's a damned liar. If the
moon's wet enough, incinerate this.

Morning

You awaken like dust
at the threshold of a breath.
Morning, cold as a stethoscope,
holds you in bed like a vase
holds a rose. What if poetry
has no place in a peaceful
world? You say, *the moon
is a lantern among birds and a bird
among lanterns.* You say,
*the moon is a window without wall
or sill.* But someone else's
midnight fills your mouth.
You say, *but we would still
have death.* And at the foundries
of worship, the workers
drop their trowels and glare
at the moon in the sky
inside your mouth. *Dolus
eventualis,* they decree when you
promise the moon is still
beautiful and death bears a baby
rattle instead of a scythe.

Bed

Here you are safe. You are safe among the ghosts
and in their absence. Safe among the white lights
and the ink. Let the white lights
be your mattress. Let the ink be your blanket.
This is the bed a ghost has made.
You be the tide to the moon's procession.
The full lung of the sea. Ghosts fill lungs like beds
of coral. You cannot drown here.
Do you breathe? The ghosts are warm and full
of love. The sea is full of love and exhales.
Look: beds drift among the waves.
A basslet shimmers. Wet stars shiver.
An ocean could drown here.
Here is a line and here is a hook.
A lure of your choosing. Throw it away.
Fishing for ghosts is like praying for love. Let the line
disintegrate. The sea is not comprised of ink.
Warm hands cup your heart. Gentle fingers rub
your larynx. The white lights and the ink
disappear. But the sea will stay.
I heard a ghost whisper, *here you are safe*
and blow away. A ghost is nibbling on your ear.

Pillow Talk

No. What you need to understand is that when I speak
of love I speak of a literal interpretation of
the word. Not of what warms itself between two
palms. Nor of what the torso's skin will speak
upon a cheek's caress. No. When I speak of love
I speak of a literal interpretation. Not of that between
a woman and a man. A man and a man. Nor
of that between the woman and the snake
who conceived a child and named her
Heaven. I do not speak of the burden of a brother
fated to flames. No. When I say love I mean it
in a literal sense. I do not speak of daisies or of lilacs
or mean to suggest the corpulence of red
or purple berries or of shadows cast in grasses
soft as cushions. I do not speak of reincarnation or
resurrection. No. I do not speak of a whale's material
heart or the ocean in any sense. No. I speak love
literally. I do not speak of the ghost of
a breath or in a breath or of a father. I do not speak
in my father's voice. When I speak of love
I do not speak. I do not speak the gust from the word.
Nor the word. I speak no letters. When I speak
of love I am prohibited to speak of it beyond
the hole in the zero that surrounds it when I speak it.

Portents

Or we are an ocean thrown across
the surface of a leaf
turning. Or all color will evaporate
like a lake where fish once
glowed and swam
like little moons, here and there.
Or cockroaches and roses
will hold communion in the fallout
of our thinking. Or the mind is
water in a wicker basket.
Or the hungry knife will be eaten
by a hematic anti-mirror.
Or what was a voice
will be replaced by a hole
whose limit is the sound of blood
moving through you like wind.
Or the last light will go out.
Or a miracle may invade
the natural. Or it is already too late.

Poem

I wanted to rescue the moon
from our hopes. I wanted
to rescue our hopes from hell.
I wanted to rescue hell
from existence. I wanted
to rescue existence
from itself.

Apologies

1. *Chrysanthemum, dying*

Or love is a firefly
smeared across the backside of an eyelid.

2. *Dear moon*

I broke you
as often as the wind is a ghost.

3. *Sparrow*

Forgive me my precision,
the tiny metal pellet in your music box.

4. *Unto poetry*

To call the heart
a pinecone, too apt, not apt enough.

I sent dead rain instead.

5. *Ashes*

Gravestones fluttered
in my lungs. I kept my tongue dark.

6. *Adjudications*

Like a song is inexorable.
Like a wren could be its only culprit.

7. *Unto nature*

In meadows I gathered
pieces of birds. I did this like a tree

assesses darkness.

8. *If not thunder*

Then moon, then moth,
then sparrow when barrenness sufficed.

9. *Caterpillar lantern*

For a poem, I wanted you
most of all. Your ghost never came back.

This inadequate scrap.

10. *Senescence*

For not confiding
in the chill these clouds resuscitate.

11. *Reconnaissance*

Your shadow-self
not mine to know, blood-red as a barn

describing snow.

12. *As a flower in early spring*

Which is to say incredulous,
imagining the soul could be circadian.

13. *As a temple*

Desire ate judgment
and grew like a hole in a tooth.

14. *Brimstone*

Hatred mistaken for love,
a palimpsest upon my burning lectern.

I buried my lanterns.

15. *What falls unsown*

Ecdysis of my penitence,
a cricket with wings resolved to soil.

16. *As a wren*

My dictums groundless
and burbling like a public fountain.

17. *Battle trance*

The song was not my own.
My violence had been inherited. It was

my own violence.

18. *Abetment*

We were as ruthless as moths.
You were a moon of tempered glass.

19. *Suppositions*

I kept them like beetles
in a terrarium polished with blood.

20. *Euouae*

Last time I visited my tomb
it looked like the world inside a mirror.

Tercets for Fear

If the lily has a song, *snow on*
the red carpet. If a song
is the cloaked thing carving

the throats out of roses, *red*
snow on the white carpet. If
the dandelion crows, *bees*

without stingers. If the crow
murders a sleeping lion, *stingers*
without bees. If daylight wears

the blade-like edges of
geranium shadows like gloves
from a lost and found, *tender*

petals fall on pebbles. If night is
a spigot unspooling its ropes
into pools among foxes

and cups, *tender pebbles grow*
on freckles. If calendars ripen
like clocks that hang from

paper walls and look like
apples, *fieldstone abatis.* If our
bodies fill with weeds, *fire*

advances. If the cellar of a lake
is riddled with videotapes
of angels making love

to demons, *window in a maze.*
If a candle is a demon's
gaze, *one wall shows another.*

Butterfly

Because a ghost
to be can be

living or yet
to live. Because

to live can mean
to ghost

through living like
the ghost I am.

Couplets for Hopelessness

I want to make a beautiful song.
A wasp is dying inside the guitar.

An early snowfall bells the trees.
The moon an untangleable yarn.

The fog is a distant bell rings apt.
Boats are burning on the river.

Two pairs of eyes erect a bridge.
The moon a moth-shaped riddle.

They say to exist is to occur forever.
Death, like sex, invents a skeleton.

Like love, an echo is usually two.
The bullet a clue nothing comes of.

Fall wears scarecrows like a rite.
Church bells dawn like bloodletting.

Prayer encircles a storm in skin.
The dead doe's black eye rippling.

We exchange pain like a currency.
My blood spins like a clock.

Birds gather like applause on wind.
Is my soul an empty mailbox?

The wind is a shawl is apt enough.
Did you name your shadow after love?

Crow and fox blood look the same.
Did you call your soul a tattered moth?

But wasn't the soul the beauty of
its own saying, form more malleable

than air? Wasn't the wind a way of
believing that the soul was there?

I once believed the soul was there.
Night is a crow pecking headstones.

My skin disguises the gore of me.
The same that hides your bones.

The Sound of Injured Rabbits

The forest I grew was impossibly dark.
I could not list the names of the trees.

Dendroidal silhouettes fled into distances
insisting, *we hold ourselves accountable for the dream.*

Two rabbits foraged a blue floor there, mutedly
luminous clearing that occurred to me

as suddenly as traps then shattered their hocks—
screams the shrill pitch of lost hearing.

As I fled, they would not fade, as if sound
could flower without wilting. I covered my ears—

the screams grew louder. I came to a hallway,
black with no mirrors, singing as I felt my way:

L is for lacunae.　　　　*A is for auriform.*
M is for mnemon.　　　　*P is for psilosis.*

The lamp I then held revealed a room where
my father reads the paper, looks up, asks

what sounds like the sound of injured rabbits?

Thistle

If in this meadow you choose
to pick a thistle in that meadow,
if in its purple pins you find
a thimble's absence in that purple,
if in this thimble you hear a wind
within that thimble's walls,
if in this wind you hear another
meadow's echo to enter, carry me
to this meadow if you would
suffer the thistle I picked for you
if in that meadow.

Sonnet

Lung—the wren's wherewithal. *Voice*—mosses changing colors
in the rain. *Spine*—tide of stones. *Memory*—a loose bone
stirring in the utter breeze. *Skin*—ignescent shadow
a forest shoulders. *Blood*—mortality grows like a tree. *Ear*—
the storm inside the cricket passes through the bedroom window.
Tooth—the moon is in the hayloft. *Mind*—raven feathers
in a wine glass. *Gut*—in a falcon's talons the snake becomes
a limp bedspring. *Liver*—dead wasps gather in the rafters.
Tongue—a mackerel casts pewter in a dark tent. *Eye*—
warped classroom window. *Heart*—a gong makes headstones
shatter. *Bone*—the chimney is a hiding place for ghosts.
Marrow—the hush is deep. *Hair*—we would climb out
through the sky. *Hand*—desperate as gravity. *Throat*—once
a holy cannon. *Soul*—the voice recedes into radiating darkness.

Voices

But it was never just the wind.   The endings to all

the saddest ghost stories always neglected
the ones disguised as other things.   As if the wind

could pass through absence and somehow speak
our names.
                                        Or massage the lip of the wine glass
that sang us blisses from an otherplace.

But physicists diagrammed the song   drew long lines
that moved like snakes   as if the humming

slithered in air around our ears while

                                        outside the wind

wove beautiful gowns of falling sleet.
But in the room with no carpet

                                        the sound of air
released from an apple's core   was louder

than the thud of an apple in grass
in the walls
                          when nothing suddenly whispered:

                james.   a name made of absence:

                                        what a ghost is.

When

When there's a wren in the bordello,
a red wine wren. When soprano

enters the voice of a shadow bled
from the ear and that shadow is

your end. When your death is just
another sentence in a sermon

so few will hear, that's when. When
the rabbit doesn't breathe in order

to breathe again. When abstractions
exhumed from the body are less

like bluebirds and more like bricks,
as concrete as imminence. When

the temple of the body splits in two,
that's when. When our skeletons

in their cellars of roots assemble
a mansion of precise silence. When

our gardens of stone outnumber
the clouds in any one sky or all

living flowers. When you lay the last
brick in the wall and that brick

is you, that's when. When the wren
comes back to beat closed the shutters.

When the final curtain is made of
wrens sewn together, struggling

to escape each other. When that
curtain's flown open and you see

your own closed eyes between
wrens trying desperately not to be

the curtain to your dying,
that'll be, that'll be, that'll be when.

Story Told to Ghosts

The foxglove said to the harebell,
wear your nightgown of existence

like a spool does, as I do. The foxglove
said to the harebell, smell sweet

like the presence of bats. The foxglove
said to the harebell, have your negligee

woven from eyelids that flutter
like curtains of a house broken into,

but the foxglove's nightgown carried it away
because it was made of flying bats.

Beggars

Violets beg with violins. Callas
beg with cups. Tulips beg

like church bells beckon. A trio
of trillium begs the question,

would we still be beautiful if
no person ever saw us? Irises

beg with the sad eyes of lilacs.
Anemones beg like a ghost

with no kitchen. Pansies beg with
soot on their faces. A choir of

spiderworts warbles, would we
be beautiful if no person ever

existed? Giant orchids beg for
nothing; they roar for it. Asters

beg with cut-rate roses. Roses
beg with thorns, receive nothing.

Transgressions

I unfurled like flora of any sort.
I poisoned myself
with milkweed, trillium, Queen
Anne's lace, or
set them in rows
less beautiful than meadows
made by birds.
I uncaged the sparrow again
and again. I flew
like the dead.
I blessed the lawn
with fireflies and blinked
a broken eye.
I set an origami crane
on fire in a garden
of roses, or released that burning
into a nightful of moons.

Ghost Logic

A rose is a rose is a rose
is a ghost. A rose arose
in the ghost of a rose.
A rose is a ghost is a rose
is a rose. A rose arose
in the rose of a ghost.
A rose is a rose is a ghost
is a rose. A rose arose
in the ghost that arose.
A ghost is a rose is a rose
is a rose. A ghost arose
in the rose that arose.

The Cat

When it sneezed
it sounded like
a small bird landing
on my shoulder—
a bird so small
it thought it had
found a mountain there
and that the wall
before me was the sky
and that the sky
beyond the window
was heaven,
for which it flew
into the glass
that shattered loud
enough to make me
jump, but it was just
the cat again,
shamefaced on top of
the table from which
a glass had fallen.

Ghosts Love Windows

Ghosts have been happening more and more
in poems lately, a phenomenon probably
having something to do with the economy,
but actually ghosts have been around for
ever, at least as long as poems, which have
been around at least forever. Ghosts,
however, are problematic in that they are,
like love, pure abstraction. As in, I love
my mother the way that ghosts are made
of sound, and love the cloud that resembles
a mushroom growing upside-down
the way the hand of my grandfather's ghost
caresses the purring cat at the foot of my bed.
If my bed had a hand, it might caress
the cat itself, in which case there would be little
need for my dead grandfather to stand
at my bed's foot while I sleep. Or, if the sky
had a mouth, I might have to settle
for an actual mushroom. Yet Ryan, wholly
afraid of the word "love," broke up with a woman
who used it to describe the way she felt
for him. And at Tuesday's reading, an audience
of mostly poets gasped when Catherine
(not a real person) told a boy she didn't love
she loved him. Such awe at such abstraction!
Yet poems are exchanging love for ghosts
without the nerve to admit how much
we are loved by them. Ghosts, the new tree.
Ghosts, the new window. And windows
love trees as much as ghosts love us,
as much as windows. Sure I use "window,"
but what does "window" really mean?

More often than not, an artificial shell
placed onto the world beyond a room, made
of glass and wood, or glass-like synthetics.
Most often, a window is a haunted magnet.
As in, ghosts love windows in old black
and white photographs, but this is the most
basic explanation—ghosts also have words
with us through windows, black and white,
ink and paper. For the time being, I am
not a medium. Our being, at this time, is likely
transcending worlds, a window between
them, a window that means, but what?
Perhaps our ghosts will one day meet,
whether we are dead or not, and be able to
explain the window to us. Perhaps we will fall
in love. I am beginning to think that Ryan
and Catherine have a lot in common
with poems, in more than one pair of ways
opposed to one another. The fun of the poem
is solving the riddle, which now seems
the poem's occasion, which it is not. But I
know that abstraction is frightening, fun, wild.
In the dark marshes of abstraction,
between the inky reeds and salivating clouds,
ghosts and poems are waiting to be found.
I watched Ryan drown in the mud there,
but I will not. And just now, as I write these
next few lines, my cat is scratching at
my window, an actual window, a window
that means, at least as much as the finches
pecking at the yard beyond it, probably more.
My cat acts like he wants to be beyond it,

but he becomes so afraid when I take him outside. In this respect, I am glad to be who I am. A cat, but not a cat. A window, but not a window. A ghost, but not a ghost. To love without fear. I feel most loved when I feel like a window a ghost is looking through.

Dinner Table Conversations

1.

I am drawn to moths as moths
are drawn to bulbs

of light   as you are
to the real world in a word

perhaps we move like wrens inflect

like obsequious mirrors
unshatter perhaps

these words can't have the accuracy
that requires one shut eye

I feel the hurt inherent in my need
to make believe

your name is a cloud
into which a wren signs mine

2.

when a tree sprang up inside the ear
I called it alder   you said pine

you tell your coworkers of my interest
in the songs ears sing when trees

inside them die   I'd like to have
time to gather

cottonwood drifts to fill my pillow

so distant screams of felled or fallen
trunks would echo

off a softer fate   as for now
my pillow brims with needles

3.

we make believe a broken tongue

play our paper violins
as thunderstorms do windows

our eyes are ears in darkrooms filled
with paper chairs

where we can hear moths flutter
like teacups   we make

believe they can hear us believe

and like to think them finicky
as wrens

but moths are not wrens
they have no beaks

our mouths feed wrens to one another
and taste exactly the same

4.

but isn't it lovely that the scent of pine
is as pleasant when limbs are still

alive   yet to better know alder
its leaves must be auburn and eaten

by fire   but isn't it better
to come to know the unspoken voices

of leaves when breezes pass through
than to risk in igniting this thicket

the cries of a warren of rabbits as it
smolders   our real words should

be as flammable as these   instead
we speak marble floors over treetops

5.

we found a garden
in the forest as we followed

bends in roads and lips   the distance
linking cusp to cup

we left no crumbs

but found this dark pariah   a garden
begotten   fronds fixated on

fricatives pillowy

as cotton   but cotton does not bud
in gardens

we bickered to the bread

or to the garden or the cotton or the cup
or to whatever

else had sung itself where it did not belong

6.

because we say the table is a field
sugar cubes in spoons turn into

divots   we speak this potpourri
into forests held in wicker

centerpieces   their brims the lips
of the clearing

lips suggesting forests being eaten

the fragrance of each basketed gasp
a consolation

from the little obliterations

our own mouths birth in casting one
another into sedges where

we become figures disfigured
dogs and orphans

who make their homes
among a pinecone's many dark pavilions

A Wren

Which is what death is:
a wren. Which is what
death makes: a song
that echoes. Which is
what we listen for:
the nearness of feathers.
Which are those that
bind us: conduits of
blood and warehouses
of air. Which is where
we begin to hunger
for the sky: inside
our bodies. Which is
where a wren collects
twigs, grass: nest-things.

Window

Two sparrows lived in separate cages
in a room, and would have been divided
from each other's view (a wall stood in
between their keeps) but for a window,
adjacent the wall, that each could look through
and upon, and see the body of the other
mirrored on its surface, that both appeared
transparent as a ghost or glass.

The window looked upon some trees, a sky,
a distant lake. The sparrows saw the scene
projected through their bodies on the glass
and believed the bodies contained its beauty
and that this beauty gave them song.
The beauty of the songs was such it caused
a longing in each bird to see the body
beyond the wall and all that each contained
together: trees, a sky, the lake that let them
sing until the quiet of rain on water.

In time the rain passed through the ceiling
over the wall, eroding it until it fell
and let each longing see its other. And so
the sparrows saw the truth was but a mirror
less like a lake than utterly unclear, a window
but an architect of ghosts, that no sky beat
within a breast nor trees within a wing.
Then rain as sudden as songs turned sad
fell quiet as the room became, and they
longed for the wall to be between them again.

Garden on the Windowsill

Facsimile lily: salmon
stargazers gaze on
Solomon's Seal
and fairybells.

Rose and rosaceous
bindweed mistaken
for violet, magenta
starfish asleep in cups.

Window to whet
whose ears are given
to eyes to wet
whose roots are fed

tears for these
distances windows
make singular: meld

of frost-blue summer
succory and tulip,
succulent colors
whose voices compel

our own to tell
of fathoms drowned
in the aloey music

of their surfaces,
each petal a fishhook
for reaping a whispery eye.

Oaks

One cannot think wrinkle
and not think surface of a face
or lake. Of time. Absence

of abstract in trees above
the green water. We cannot skip
an acorn like a stone. We

are thirsty, grateful we cannot
cup this wrinkled bark
like water in our hands, sip.

Green water, perennial dark,
black of trunks the only
fact that lets us know the sky

is deeply blue when clear
and dark. We sit on the dock
above the lake, the trees

behind us, a distant storm
across the lake. Perennial blue
light and quiet thunder,

crickets, wind. We know
the trees are there. They shiver
as if a ripple paused mid-rift.

The Body before the Judgment

Having not yet sprouted wings for flight
through everlight

                moths flocking

an incandescent bulb at night

Lakes of dead moths pool in streetlights
forming eyes

along dark shoreline wonder
are these leaves

the ghostly friction of wind and tree

hanging against the moonbeam
what will be

                Mist sifting

the emptiness over the lake

below a sky we ran the oakwood dock
where spiderwork

was torn apart with sticks the trees
had dropped to tempt us

into tattered webbings draped
and shaking with

                writhing moths

The bobber cast from water's sill

still as the surface allowed until the worm
was drowned

but it's been buried all its life
you said and tied it to

the loose string of a helium balloon

ascended to a temple made from cloud
and mirrored on the lake

Midge clouds over clouds reflected

thresholds on a patch of ripples
algae marred and
                    brimming seaweed

our motor chopped through into waters
dark and deep

and moth legs clung the Kevlar hull

as we did the rim of sleep
against the motorhum

across above the lake we cut through
a mirror
                    a temple torn into

Rhymes for the Cat's Ashes

1.

A wren as if a cup of blood.
Its song as if the ghost of prayer.

Its flight as if to herald floods.
Its soul as if to nest in hair.

2.

When moonlight like a boat appears
in a fraction of sky far less than half

its whole and fogs the bay
window where you curled and slept

I think, if you had been the moon
the moon's fur would have shuddered

a deep and quiet ease at the touch
of my hand. But I have never touched

the moon death proves is a cliché,
apt and indispensable. "I can't

believe the snow is gone like nothing
happened," she said the day

when everything became a never-again.

3.

Tiny breaking moon.
Hand mirror swoon.

Thought she saw
the dead cat paw

the curtain in the room
behind the room.

4.

Bird bones in a cricket cage—
you've returned from the sky!

We know because the spoon's
misplaced, the crumb's erased,

all time is due, the crickets
are preaching to the moon

that cannot be saved or sung
anew, its sorrow settling

in the room, where murmurs
turned about your face.

5.

Night sounds like crickets.
Tiny breaking windows.

The wolf threads her hunger
through deep dewy thickets

as a bittern finds a minnow
under the moon.

6.

Cue the lullaby, you moon
askew, you pocketed tuffet

of rye the sky coveted,
silver as toebells or feathers

to fiddle, night-gathered
wool, you soul made of rags,

your haystacks all riddles,
your cockleshell gaze, lip

of infinity, candlesticks
dwindle, the kettle-flue's

muted, treetops forsaken
by cradles gnaw hushes,

ashes are ashes, our teeth
window sashes, grinding

the rye of you, trivial bread
blistered in looking-glass

castles as vast as our dark
gullet corridors, lullaby dead.

7.

An egg as if a tear escaped.
A nest as if to cradle hope.

A branch as if to balance fate.
A gust as if to bare the yolk.

8.

If a tempestuous wolf gallops over
the moonlit clover

If she slavers at trees beyond
the forest of clover

And the only snow
is the canopy's

If a moonlit moth
is the tempest's lung

If she drops her snow over
dust beneath the canopy

And the only wind
is a dying lung's

If I had not run from the forest's rim
into deeper trees

If the wolf's appetite is not for trees
but for my song

And the only lyrics
are my last

9.

That the rose in the mirror
is no less real than the rose

says of sight…

That an echo is more
beautiful than its source

says of sound…

That tingling in the wake of a hand's
graze is never less beautiful than

the hand says of touch…

That I find myself at the window caressing
and warbling to a little wooden box says

of soul…

10.

A wing as if to cup the moon.
A boat as if to rereturn.

A roost of light the night cocoons.
A chirp as if to spill the urn.

11.

But each night, distance comes
like a wolf upon a warren,

quiet as a closing eye, hinging
dark to darkness. Humming

porch lights paint screen doors
with blurry moths. Warm

screams pursued by darknesses
that through snow rummage

for the glow of those doomed
kingdoms are born in a room

of soil and root, faraway bells,
skies elided. My cold hands swell

like the distance and stroke
the fur of a deeper shadow:

night—wolf dusted with snow,
the blacks of her eyes growing

as she bites into the hereafter.

Hope

For the crickets whose death
your voice becomes. For the grace of lunchtime

moons. For the veil of dark, dying elms
that rumor low, *your heart will not endure you.*

When your soul feels caught, like a flag sounds.
When the sky is an urn turned inside-out.

When your love is returned like a library book
but with words crossed out.

And revere what cannot reciprocate.
And bow like crickets to the meadows.

And evaporate like moths to moonlight.
You'll be palaced in sky like a kinglet.

You'll bend like time around each tree
trunk and limb and leaf and bird. You'll nestle

like a lullaby. I will stop the day that I
inhale a dragonfly, and neither of us gets hurt.

Answers

Tree because it cannot seize the moon.
Leaf because it cannot sing
your fate. Worm
because the scent of rain came as sudden
as the rain. Bird because
the broken shells
were once the shapes of lungs.
Ghost because your ticking heart
would sooner die than stop.
Light because it cherishes
the shadows it soaks up. Forest floor
because the dead invent religions
made of moss. Hidden
door because our ghosts forget
how to fashion song
from loss. Beauty because spiders turn
trees to mummified chandeliers.
Love because the end is always near.

Hallway

we heard the echo down the hallway down the hall
way down the hall we heard the echo down the
hallway down the hall way down we chased the
echo down the hallway down the hall way down
the hall we chased the echo down the hallway
down the hall way down we caught the echo down
the hallway down the hall way down the hall we
caught the echo down the hallway down the hall

way down we laced the echo down the hallway
down the hall way down the hall we laced the echo
down the hallway down the hall way down we
wore the echo down the hallway down the hall way
down the hall we wore the echo down the hallway
down the hall way down we were the echo down
the hallway down the hall way down the hall
we were the echo down the hallway down the
whole way down

Door

There could be a stairwell that leads to a cellar where
there are screams beyond a door whose mouth is closed.
A cellar with screams that find a door whose jaw is locked.
There could be many open jaws from which screams leave
a cellar the jaws cannot. There could be a cellar whose jaws
are locked. A furnace whose mouth is open. There is a door
and beyond a door there could be a room with many
floors. A furnace from which screams find a door whose
jaw is locked. Whose mouth is closed. There could be a door
beyond a door behind which screams are louder than we
thought. But there is a door. There is and are a door and
screams beyond a door we can remember. There is the way
the word for door becomes the name of a demon when
repeated. A demon whose mouth we cannot remember.
Whose mouth we cannot enter. There could be a well-fed
furnace beyond a door whose mouth is closed. A furnace
who feeds a burning well. Furnace within a further furnace.
Furnace whose jaws are locked. There is and are a door and
screams beyond what could be. A door with many mouths.
A mouth with many doors. A well-fed well or chimney
whose smoke is blocked. Whose jaw is locked. Whose neck
is wrought. There could be. But the door and the screams
are enough to wake us. To know there is pleasure behind it.

Porch

there are traces of a suicide
in every moth
that ventures from the night
for lanterns burning
in the cul-de-sac

where we sought relief
beneath the rain
of particles
of moths that beat themselves
against the porch light

until we were sheltered
behind masks of moth dust
that we might have blended
into the corners
where dead skin gathers

to rise only by moon
with our handfuls of dust
which we would press into
the hot glass
to dampen the light

of this altar
to the world of not quite
resurrection
where the dust that rises from
wings must settle because

there are traces of a moth
in every suicide

The Moon

The moon is not a goddess. It is
no mother, wears no bodice.

There is no man in it, nor
an eye. The moon

is not a drum
and sings no child to sleep.

The moon is not a wayfarer
or wafer. It has no congregation of stars

or otherwise. The moon
has not been hung, nor is it

a hook from which to hang.
The moon is not a plate

or shell. It is not the bottom of a well.
It is not salt and has no fat,

is not a grain of any kind.
The moon cannot be swallowed,

knows nothing of fate.
It is not made of silver light,

nor does it raise
wolves, ravens, moths,

or horses, whose hooves have never hewn
paths across its craters.

This is not a poem about the moon.

Lilies

My inheritance is the names
of flowers, my tongue
a red headstone speaking
the names of lilies. My
inheritance is the names of
flowers, my tongue a red
headstone speaking the names
of lilies. My inheritance
is the names of flowers,
my tongue a red headstone
speaking the names of lilies.
Our inheritance is the names
of flowers, our tongues
red headstones speaking
the names of the lilies.

Notes

"Ghost Logic" is after Gertrude Stein.

Section 2 of "Dinner Table Conversations" responds, in part, to the first of Rilke's *Sonnets to Orpheus*.

The words "climb out through the sky" in "Sonnet" come from Barry Lopez's short story "Buffalo."

photo by: Elizabeth Threadgill

James Henry Knippen grew up in the suburbs of Chicago and received his MFA from Texas State University. He is the recipient of a 92Y Discovery Prize. His poetry has appeared in *32 Poems, AGNI, Colorado Review, Crazyhorse, Denver Quarterly, Gulf Coast, The Kenyon Review Online,* and *West Branch,* among other journals. He is the poetry editor of *Newfound.*

The New Issues Poetry Prize

James Henry Knippen, *Would We Still Be*
2020 Judge: Traci Brimhall

Daniel M. Becker, *2nd Chance*
2019 Judge: Jericho Brown

Chet'la Sebree, *Mistress*
2018 Judge: Cathy Park Hong

Nina Puro, *Each Tree Could Hold a Noose or a House*
2017 Judge: David Rivard

Courtney Kampa, *Our Lady of Not Asking Why*
2016 Judge: Mary Szybist

Sawnie Morris, *Her, Infinite*
2015 Judge: Major Jackson

Abdul Ali, *Trouble Sleeping*
2014 Judge: Fanny Howe

Kerrin McCadden, *Landscape with Plywood Silhouettes*
2013 Judge: David St. John

Marni Ludgwig, *Pinwheel*
2012 Judge: Jean Valentine

Andrew Allport, *the body | of space | in the shape of the human*
2011 Judge: David Wojahn

Jeff Hoffman, *Journal of American Foreign Policy*
2010 Judge: Linda Gregerson

Judy Halebsky, *Sky=Empty*
2009 Judge: Marvin Bell

Justin Marks, *A Million in Prizes*
2008 Judge: Carl Phillips

Sandra Beasley, *Theories of Falling*
2007 Judge: Marie Howe

Jason Bredle, *Standing in Line for the Beast*
2006 Judge: Barbara Hamby

Katie Peterson, *This One Tree*
2005 Judge: William Olsen

Kevin Boyle, *A Home for Wayward Girls*
2004 Judge: Rodney Jones

Matthew Thorburn, *Subject to Change*
2003 Judge: Brenda Hillman